Send Cows to Kevin's Mom

Ricky Braun

BookLeaf
Publishing
India | USA | UK

Presentation by *BookLeaf Publishing*

Web: www.bookleafpub.com

E-mail: info@bookleafpub.com

ISBN: 978-93-5744-786-7

First edition 2022

DEDICATION

The secret of life is fresh cilantro, thank you to
all of you who believed in me up till now

ACKNOWLEDGEMENT

I acknowledge the land I currently reside on is Treaty 1 Territory, traditional territory of the Anishinaabeg, Cree, Oji-Cree, Dakota, and Dene Peoples, and on the homeland of the Métis Nation.

Disclaimer: if you want to read a book that makes sense— this book is not it.

PREFACE

"Eventually, something you love is going to be taken away. And then you will fall to the floor crying. And then, however much later, it is finally happening to you: you're falling to the floor crying thinking, "I am falling to the floor crying," but there's an element of the ridiculous to it — you knew it would happen and, even worse, while you're on the floor crying you look at the place where the wall meets the floor and you realize you didn't paint it very well. "

- Richard Siken

Hitchhiking Strangers (i.)

In a city of everything coated in identical plaid
blue shirts,
I am standing over there,
in the neon-orange-carrot costume.
Are we strangers?

Do you believe that hair is a personal plant you
get at birth for free and all you have to do is
water it sometimes and wash it sometimes and
then it grows forever?
Do you believe in god, or do you believe that
shuffle knew exactly what song you needed to
hear?
If i guessed your password would it be
"Ihatepasswords123"?

There are a variety of places in the world that do
not use toilet paper, and there are also people
who do use toilet paper. What if the place that
makes toilet paper is in a place that does not use
toilet paper? What if one time the factory

machine forgot to add the
for-ripping-dotted-lines for 27 squares?

What if your computer was a spherical shape,
and when you played baseball with it, anytime
you got a home run, it would automatically do a
google image search of people sticking their
head in a freezer?

Would it make more sense to change the
hemispheres from time to time instead of
Daylight savings?

If I had a condition in which I was deathly
scared of corduroy, I would then force everyone
else on earth to wear corduroy so I wouldn't
have to talk to anyone ever again.

Hitchhiking Strangers (ii.)

Dear Strangers Who've Loved Me Right Away,
you must know you are a rare but vital part of
this world.

You frighten me; I stare at you in disbelief and
wonder how your heart got so accepting.

You're the exact the opposite of me. Yet here we
go, hand in hand, strangers to soul-knowers
within a few hours. So you might have loved me
right away, and as quickly as you did, also
forgotten me, but
you leave me knowing I'll never forget you.

You somehow tattooed yourself on me without
my permission, and my brain seems to recall
every word you said to me, bringing it back to
me in the late, late night when I'm falling asleep
on the bus home.

Dear Strangers Who've Loved Me Right Away-
when I fall to my worst of being deserving of
you,
you face-plant smack-dab in the middle of my
life…at what always seems to be " just the right
time" …

Dear Strangers Who've Loved Me Right Away,
I'm sorry that I couldn't give you back the
immediate love your heart required in the
moment,
but yours was overwhelming,
that all I could do was stand frozen.
As a human without a home,
as a dreamer,
 as one with tremendous fascination of unseen
magic in the air:
I depend on you,
I long to meet you, and
I keep the light on my heart balcony on at night
for you.
For your unending dedication
to pursue friendship with me without reason,
for your "not-giving-up" or letting me go so
quickly—
You have taught me how to put trust in someone,
(There was no time to convince myself
otherwise.)

Hitchhiking Strangers (iii.)

"Life is soup, I am a fork"- Pakalu Papito

Meet me at a quarter after 9
Meet me at the convenient store
Tell me i'm not as great as flipping burgers as i
think i am
Tell me i'm better at
not flipping out when i accidentally get on the
wrong train

Tell me that we sure have gone through a lot
together
Tell me a reminder that i ran out of coffee filters
so we need to take a short cut home
Tell me that when the sunlight shows every dust
particle in the air, i am not allergic to the stuff i
claim to be.

Tell me that 5 years ago was the last time a
telephone pole set on fire and it watched as i did
nothing to stop it

Tell me, why can some people not get past their
struggle in the moment and can not
communicate, even when it is vital? (which feels
like the polar express)
This is hard to express except there is nothing
you can do,
you can't force people to be different on the
inside.

Tell me that i could have everything in my room
imported from the Netherlands and i
still would not feel as important as the last time i
drank in a graveyard listening to my favourite
radio station.
Tell me, are they watching us from space?
Tell me that your roommate might be dropping
your toothbrush in the toilet accidentally and not
telling you
so
make sure you have something rosy to mask the
pain.
Tell me that, as long as there's no more plastic
water bottles, expensive and extensive breakfast
specials and
poles without fish, life can go on without
anybody noticing the bigger picture.
Tell me that i'm still alive,
I'll tell you to not doubt me.

Meet me in the middle of website browsing
pages coming and going,

forgotten anniversaries coming and going,

Aqua Magic Laundry customers coming and
going.

It is the same place where
love comes and goes—
it's just nice when it happens.

Gas Station Coffee (i.)

How can you fix a car if it's broken but you insist that you like it that way? How many suspicious white bumps are on your wall? Let's talk about whether you like the colours of astronaut space suits or birds nests on top of telephone poles. Let's not talk at all if you only look at the world while wearing swimming goggles your parents bought you when you were 7.

Let's talk about many Gas stations are there in Fiji? A "glass is half empty" outlook on life would be a great asset to working at a gas station. It's hard to research the total number of gas stations in Fiji because their gas stations are all named TOTAL.

(I think there is 10.)

Let's talk if you sometimes see that poofy clouds have creatures hiding behind them, with your binoculars. Let's talk about the most amount of long johns you can fit under your pants at one time, and if that number reflects the weather, or the size of your pants?

Let's talk about why don't our ears sneeze and
why do some birth parents tell you they don't
love you anymore?

Gas Station Coffee
(ii.)

There was once a rock among other rocks,
laying on the side of the path.
One day, it caught the eye
of someone passing by.

With a spark of intrigue
(or perhaps a lazy day)
the rock was picked up to be admired—
for it looked quite different and contrastingly
peculiar.

However, to the collectors' surprise,
as it was lifted,
an unexpected discovery was made.

What a heavy rock!
With the weight of the world,
this rock was far too heavy to handle.

The stranger began to feel
the impractical strain this rock gave.

No sooner had the rock been picked up, was it
ready to be discarded.
(No longer worthy be held)

The stranger shrugged, looking out at the river
below.
The rock would, be perfect for throwing off the
bridge.

And with that, the rock left the hand of beholder
plummeting through the air,
abruptly breaking the river's surface.

Submerging through the murky water,
lower and lower the rock sank
with all of its substantial weight.

Sinking down to the bottom,
the rock settled itself on the river beds' floor—

and to the rocks' surprise
she was surrounded by
all the other interesting looking rocks, carrying
the weight of the world.

Gas Station Coffee (iii.)

Imagine one morning you woke up in "Crab Park" (which is actually called Crack park) in between two rather large street signs that formed a sort of tent.
It was the gloomy kind of morning, where all you want to do is not tie your shoes
but instead eat blueberries,
and see how far you can throw them while sitting on the edge of the dock at Crack park.
With only old impark tickets for liter, and not a squawking bird in flight yet,
your sleepy stare crosses over each miniature dock house and boat. When you are in-between jobs,
time in the morning passes rather slowly—and makes sure you ponder if you were meant to be a sailor and if it's best to find out the truth before its too late?
But your wonderings disappear promptly.
For the clouds begin to hover even lower, as if to try and hinder the day from it's inevitable pace.

The breeze across the water rushes in as if its'
slept in
and the morning calm quickly turns to ripples
and triples your desire for when you could
obtain the next available cup of coffee.

Listening To am Radio (i.)

What if your favourite author,
wrote your favourite book,
even when if he hadn't been to the hairdresser in
quite some time?
And he wrote parts in his car,
because he kept forgetting his keys inside before
he left the house?

What if your favourite artist,
sculpted your favourite piece
in the back alley of a grocery store,
since her home was cluttered with too many
items she collected?
And she hadn't washed her bed sheets in
months?
And insomnia let her only sculpt in the evening,
without natural light (even though that is
bothersome?)

What if, your favourite athlete,
forgot to drink enough water the day of their
game in the finals?

Or went weeks without calling their
grandparents,
and now they realize they're too old to say much
anymore, so
they try to make up for years of lost time (in
packed minutes of the day)

So timing is never perfect.
My train ride ended but my playlist still had 2
more songs.
Your alarm clock rings at a different time than
mine.
And it's only coincidence we ever collided.
It's only coincidence the wind blew my bus
transfer out of my gum packet wallet and I had
to run down the street in the other direction to
get it.
It's only coincidence that we met
on the bench outside.
I forgot to tell you,
I was running late.
Is that fate?

Listening To am Radio (ii.)

The sense of touch gets a bad rep for all the ways in which it can be abused. But you know in the dark when you can't see anything so you have to rely on "feeling" the couch to the wall to the door to the light switch?

I give my extremely-sensitive-emotional-self a bad rap most of the time and let myself and others abuse it.
My life went pitch black, and
feelings were the only thing to rely on to get through the dark to find the light switch.

Listening To am Radio (iii.)

Some trees are tall
Some trees are small
and some trees keep standing even after they're
dead.
They said
"even though I weathered many bad storms in
my life,
and am now pronounced dead,
I am still standing.
So who do you think really won."

Do not send me a postcard with your return
address on it.
Instead leave me a bag of ketchup chips on my
windshield or
write me a temporary message in the snow on
my windshield.

Just so I don't have to keep a letter forever
On the inside pocket of my Jean jacket.

I will reply
When I can
With a sharpie note on the backseat of the #11
bus

Matching Hairstyles
(i.)

The air is soft
no matter the time
sitting under a vine
(i cling to your arm)

A man bikes by
you gave him a dollar
he gave you sparkling water
(with a lemon slice)

The sun shines,
i readjust my cap
from the bench where we sat
(you throw the wedge)

•

i jog alone through the park
a couple years later
i no longer hold anger
(i step on something squishy)

i scrap off the dirt
i readjust my thoughts
if we hadnt have fought
(i might still live here)

Maybe i left a bit of me

in Battery Park

i once hugged the ground

where you walked

Life swiftly moves onward

and you have forgot it

a plane flies through the

sky, i look up to watch it

Life is fragile, delicate, brittle and crisp

Life is perishable and often run-down to its' last
bits

but the dirt off my shoe

touched the lemon seed you threw—

and that's why there's a Lemon tree
Growing in Battery Park

Matching Hairstyles (ii.)

How can I catch you if you
Aren't falling in my direction?
Or If my body isn't strong enough?
Or If my arms are caught in my sleeve?

How can I feel safe?
Must I surround myself with only soft textures?
Like silk or holiday tinsel
Or petting a dogs ear?

How does sadness turn to happiness?
If I counted all the times I thought of running
away,
counted all the times I didn't mean what I say,
I was trying but the words came out all wrong.

How do i make monthly bill payments go by
slower?
What if borrow your vacuum tomorrow?
Youtube helps me focus,
because the music stops playing if you close the
tab.

How can I remember the last conversation we
had
What if my eyelids stayed open
And my 7/11 never closed
And every door of every room must be
decorated with different doorknobs?

Matching Hairstyles
(iii.)

Ich dachte, ich hätte dich heute gesehen
in einer Schuhwerbung

Ich schwöre, ich habe dich heute gesehen,
auf Gleis 7,
bis der Zug meine Augen blockiert.

Ich dachte, ich hätte dich gesehen
durch den kleinen Park neben der Hauptstraße
gehen
(bin ich sicher!)

ich dachte, ich hätte dich gesehen, wie du in der
Bäckerei Zwiebelbrot zum Mitnehmen bestellt
hast (das war dein jackett…wirklich!)

ich dachte, ich hätte dich in den Linien gesehen,
auf die Wand meiner Dusche zeichnen und

ich dachte definitiv, ich hätte dich gesehen, als
du dein Fahrrad vor dem Netto aufgeschlossen
hast

Ich dachte, ich hätte dich ganz sicher gesehen.
(es ist total egal, dass du nicht mehr hier
wohnst... du würdest einen Weg
finden…zurückzukommen)

um mich mitten am Tag anhalten zu lassen und
meinen Hals so weit zu verrenken, dass ich von
der Treppe falle
oder darüber zu lachen, dass mein Auto vergisst,
den Kreisverkehr zu verlassen

Du bringst mein Herz dazu mich auf der Straße
anzuhalten und mein herz fragt ob ich eine
zusätzliche Zigarette habe

ich dachte, ich hätte dich nachts am
Dachbodenfenster gesehen, Zähneputzen

Ich glaube, ich bin mir sicher, dass es unmöglich
ist…so viele Doppelgänger zu haben

Flat Tire, Where's Bucks Auto? (i.)

A penguin and an alien were sitting on a pumpkin in park one day in late September.

The penguin turned to the alien and asked "How old are you, Alien?"

"I'll be 1,002 tomorrow." said the Alien.

"That is quite a lot of birthdays."
the Penguin responded. "I wish I had that much experience, living to 1,000 and traveling to other planets."

The Alien looked up and down and replied, "Well, I wish I had your shoes."

The Penguin glanced at his combat boots and said "You know, you could get them too, at the store down the street. There's probably a pair in your size, waiting for you to walk by."

The Alien grinned.

"And you," started the Alien "could read another book. And take on new challenges no matter what your age. You could try to swim all the way to India. You do not ever have to have the same career your whole life. You do not have to listen to other penguins. You don't have to speak the same language your whole life. You could try to learn cow, or dog, or an alien language, perhaps. I hear there is plenty of different foods in the sea. You don't have to save up all your money just to keep it in a snowbank all your life. The ocean is out there; but there is also a whole world just down your street. There is colours in the back alley you've never seen before. There is a neighbour behind your house who has the same cookbook as you and could share with you a secret to glazing squid. There's a tree in this park about 50 meters from us right now that is very rare and hidden. Do you know it's kind? There is an embroidery shop with a grandma penguin who sits on her balcony twice a day and has told me what hairstyle I should try next. We also play crib on Sundays sometimes. Have you met her yet?

The penguin stared blankly.

The Alien noticed that most of this had gone over the penguins' head; and that his Alien-ramblings had once again taken flight without anyone looking up in the sky to wish them farewell.

„Ah well" the Alien sighed. "Experience is not just the years allotted to your life here on earth. It is about how much you open yourself up to it, and if you desire to continually learn."

"How do you say Happy Birthday in your language?" asked the Penguin.

"https://m.youtube.com/watch?v=IESy6GbD-vg " said the Alien.

Flat Tire, Where's Bucks Auto? (ii.)

Sometimes I wish the electricity between two
people could charge my ipod or make my wifi
faster.
Sometimes if i think about it,
don't a lot of humans resemble turtles? (maybe
it's just a seasonal thing.)
Sometimes you try to facetime me but i dropped
my ipod in ketchup while watching the jets
game last week.
Sometimes people stop me on the street to say,
"Describe to me aliens, mermaids, and ghosts"
And i ask, do you mean by states of matter:
aliens are solid, mermaids are liquid and ghosts
are gas.

Sometimes my honey sinks down to the bottom
of my tea.
Sometimes my paintings take too many tries.
Sometimes my heart sinks down to my feet.
and it's hard to walk.
Sometimes things take time.

Sometimes my life takes a downward turn.
Sometimes i hit the ground too fast.
Sometimes cold pizza is better.
Sometimes the best things are last.

Sometimes I am an owl,
and as i look all around me,
I have found only one way to really change the
world:
If you hold any power over making sure what
hurt you yesterday, doesn't hurt someone else
today, then use it.
If there is any given chance for you to change
the outcome of someone elses' circumstance,
(because you went through the same thing- only
the bad version) and you help them so that the
bad version does not happen to them, take that
chance.
Because if i say "Well i received that pain
unknowingly, then so should they"
the world might stay the same.

Flat Tire, Where's Bucks Auto? (iii.)

The last pink puff of cloud
in the sunset tonight
hangs on a little longer
Pulls your heart towards breaking

The fragile pure piano note
in the song tonight
hangs in mid air a little longer
Pulls your lungs from breathing

The quiet sense that
you're not here tonight
hangs in the room
I wished you could have, stayed a little longer

The softness of your eyes
in my mind tonight
hangs only in my memory
I'll pull the blanket a little bit closer

When you finally get home,
after a long hard life

Hang your hat a little longer—
Everything was meant to be.

A bird perched on a tiny twig
in the winter tree tonight
hangs on the bare branch a little longer—
Life is just, a fleeting moment.

How To Forget Someone (i.)

Why is the aftermath so much harder than real math?

Raise your hand if you razor your hands because you assume most swimming pools aren't deep enough to touch the bottom.
Razor your hands if you raise your hand in front of a deer in the headlights when your innerself leans towards the optimistic side of a 51 % chance you got the signal for a high five.
Be efficient, tomorrow you could wake up to all your planted gardens demolished at the scene.
Be efficient, if you walk around with a brown paper bag over your head, (at least it's not plastic) you still won't be able to see which way you're looking when you cross the road.

The bus won't hit you, if you provide the attiquite amount of old bus tickets and lint.

And if it is accepted as correct payment, the bus
driver will take you on a guided tour-adventure
through eternity.
They will tell you over the intercom that the
opposite of time and space is infinity and all the
letters on a chessboard.

They will tell you over the intercom that if your
brain has run out of stuff to overthink about, and
you feel every backwards slidestep of your
slippery organ collapsing into itself, there is a
cure.
Or if your brain has happened to have gone past
the point of no return and the quick sand quickly
turned into a black hole of mud where you no
longer can see foreseeable help in the future,
there is a cure.
Or might be, your brain has turned against you
as if you hadn't already promised it a limitless
use of a loyality card with all the stamps filled
out that never expires,
there is a cure.
(See if you have an emergency five dollar bill in
your sock that you can use to help you not think
about IT.
If 5 dollars is all the willpower you have left,
and if you are down to your last straw and it is
not biodegradable,

or if the mud of the black hole has now sunk into
every inbetween area of your brain— there is
still a cure.

At the red light, the bus driver will tell you that
in two hours or two days or two months or two
decades this feeling might be over. However
right now, even two seconds feels impossible to
get through,
there is a cure.

We are traveling to infinity.
Look out the window.

How To Forget Someone (ii.)

I love the way people move back and forth when
they're playing the piano.

If you really want to forget someone, let's try to
forget this question.
Roll it onto a stick of seaweed,
place it inside a shell,
balance it on a waves edge,
and let the water carry it away.

Because you didn't litter,
you dont have to do anything with it anymore.
Run to the nearest tallest tree you can find.
(for me it's my sister)
When you get to the top,
recall a song about a cat who was also a poptart.
(maybe sing along)
Please resist the urge to write
"still listening to the current year" as a comment
down below.
Take a souvenir leaf from this tree, form a
pocket in your sock and turn it into an

emergency 5 dollar bill because you'll need that
for later.

Walk down the street and
On your way, wave to the guy in the yellow
shirt.
If he waves back, ask him directions to his
favourite bar.
And once you get there, inspect all the stools
and chairs to see which one is worn in the most.
Found it?
You now sit on a musical chair of a stranger who
choses to wear yellow shirts in public.
Grab a drink if you haven't already and think
about all the grocery lists you've seen lying on
the ground without owners.
Contemplate if they were already used for their
worthy cause or if they were forgotten before
they fulfilled their purpose...
Just before you leave— why don't you pull out
your house key to scratch the initials of the first
concert you ever went to on the bottom of this
musical chair.

Go outside and turn in the direction towards
home.
Do you smell that?
It's two people who can't decide what pizza
flavour is the worst.

Go tell them to get Pinapple without the ham
and extra jalapeños.
And now you've made it past all the
neighbourhoods with tree-named streets, you are
almost home.
Three more cracks in the sidewalk till you've
made it.
After you've brushed all your teeth,
Right before you fallen asleep,
reach into your sock and take out the leaf which
is also a 5 dollar bill currency.

Sit on your windowsill
and look at the sky.
The 2 am freeze will tell you:
This $5 leaf is on the brink of its life,
and you might be too.
Don't give up.

Tonight, leave your bed sheets a little shorter,
so your feet stick out and the frost will bite your
toes while you are sleeping.
Any bad life decisions you try to make in your
dreams will be prevented,
since you'll get cold feet.

How To Forget Someone (iii.)

Maybe if you remember every memory 10 times over,
Your free trial will run out and
You will get the chance to cancel your
subscription before paying

Maybe if you squeeze your eyes as tight as you can
And forget that they taught you how to drive
And forget the field you used to run to get away from them
And forget the string that is still on their wrist

Maybe if you stay up as late as you can-
Past the last train,
Past the two am delivery man,
Past the secret time 24/7 shops close…

Only there will
the haunting, the ghost and the hurt
be trapped and locked outside.

There you will have made it
To the other side
Of forgetting.

Try Again Tomorrow (i.)

Reinventing my surroundings every month,
Rearranging my words, biting my tongue
Paralyzingly emotions since I was young
Stuff I was told I'm not allowed to become

(Im trying to be who I once was,
Trying not to be who I once was)

Smelling like smoke and familiar perfume
Dreading what happens in the afternoon
Telling a boy about loving a girl
In my previous life, in Saskatoon

(Trying to be who I once was
Trying not to be who I once was)

If I don't fold my own laundry, no one will
If I don't set my own boundaries, no one will
I could grow old, fooled by uncertainty,
Still no one will
Tell you how to be free

(Trying to be who I once was
Trying not to be who I once was)

Harmony is: radiating through me
Despite your disapproval of me
You got me prayin for my enemies
Harmony is: not disappointing me

Last November feels nothing
like this November
Every year I grow a new winter coat
unrecognizable is an antidote

(So im trying to be who I once was
And I'm trying not to be who I once was)

My hope is
You can be You
And Ican be me

Whatever
that may end up to be

Try Again Tomorrow (ii.)

I believe holidays are only for people with
families, which is why I find the use of
hanging-lights much better for a clothes line.
Do you have a favourite side you chew your
gum on first?
For me it's the left, since all my teeth on the
right have fallen out.
Although missing teeth scares me to death,
What's worse is finding fuzz in my backpack i
didn't know was there.
And at the same time,
finding out guests are coming over later.

When guests come to my house,
(which i spray painted myself)
I like to pour them all bowls of cereal, and
casually tell them I forgot to buy milk.
Then I run away immediately,
leaving all my belongings in my spray painted
house behind.
The only things I have time to grab is your old
phone case

and my Karaoke Machine.
I move across the world,
back to the town I was born in where no one
knows my real name.
I will settle into the barren desert that offers
suitable & affordable dental healthcare
and there continue my life, scare-free.

Happy Halloween

The Beginning, The End, And The Cockroach Who Joined The 27 Club

I'll burn my tongue again, still too hot
Not looking down the street, I'll run across
I'm not afraid of getting caught
And I am not afraid of the loss

I've lived my whole life walking
foot in front of foot along the edge,
The gasps are familiar as they watch
my choices dangle over the ledge

Since I was small they've tried to tell me
That I'm "wise in my own eyes"
They never told me those were lies
They never told me everyone dies

Is this possible to see?
There is no sense in trying to change me.
I will never learn the safest way to be,

and I will never start trying to please

you.

But, people find that out about me too late.
That I throw higher & higher at all the stakes.
That I dangerously bet on my life before it's
done—

I guess thats why I'm always cooking for one

www.ingramcontent.com/pod-product-compliance
Lightning Source LLC
Chambersburg PA
CBHW070607160726
48003CB00005B/2143